# IMAGINE
## (Chronicles Of an Urban School Principal)

Photos by Troy (T-Roy) Jones

Copyright © 2021 by Jerri A. Johnson

Names have been changed to protect the people I have written about, whether innocent or guilty. The only thing I did not change are my true chronicles as a school principal — IMAGINE THAT!

The opinions expressed in this book are those solely of the author and do not reflect the opinions of Million Words Publishing or its Editors.

Thank you.

Published By:
Million Words Publishing, LLC
Enjoyed By You!
WORDS THAT LAST FOREVER!®
www.millionwordspublishing.com

Library of Congress Catalog Card Number:
ISBN #: 978-1-891282-25-6

**Imagine That!**
Printed in the United States of America

# TABLE OF CHRONICLES

## Acknowledgements

First, I must give honor to God for all that He has done in my life and putting it on my heart to write this book. It has been years of doubting that anyone would want to hear my story, because I felt that I was not important enough or I'm not accomplished enough to write a book. During the pandemic, I experienced a layoff (#7 in my career) and writing this book weighed heavy on my heart. With double digit years in the field of education, my family and friends have seen me go through it all. I want to thank them from the bottom of my heart, for encouraging me and supporting me through this life journey.

My daughter, however, has experienced everything firsthand, by living with me daily and seeing all of the challenges that I have weathered in her 19 years on this earth. When I finished my Doctorate degree and was so tired that I didn't even want to go to the ceremony, she was the one who told me I HAD to walk across the stage because I had been in school all her life. LOL, it was hilarious! She had endured all the layoffs, the two divorces, the various jobs, and positions that I held. She also knew that when that graduation morning came, I had cried in my bathroom before I came out to see her with a smile on my face. My daughter has been my motivating force to FINISH everything that I have started in this life. I will NOT fail in front of her, but I will always learn the lesson. I love you to life sweetie!

To all my educator colleagues/friends, this book would not have been written without you. Everyone that has entered my life in the field of Education has been an inspiration, good or bad. All in all, I love you guys, even though you may have driven me NUTS! Keep doing what you are doing. Our kids need you! Every person that you meet won't appreciate you, but I **absolutely** do!

Parents, as parents, we don't always get it right. You have motivated me as well. Just know that educators listen to you. But we need you to listen to us also. If it weren't for you, we wouldn't exist. We know that, and we are here to help!

**Let's Do This Together!**

# Introduction

Imagine that you are the principal of a predominately black school in an urban area. What images come to mind? The life of any school principal is that of constant uncertainty, modification, and adaptation. School principalship is a demanding job for anyone who decides to take on the challenge. However, that life being compounded with the needs and requirements that come along with leading a predominantly black school in an urban area makes it even more challenging, yet worthwhile. People may say that all school principals have the same accountability and frustrations that come along with the job. In reality, that is just not true! From my perspective, urban schools have had more accountability and scrutiny than other schools. Also, from my perspective, a suburban school principal with little to no students of color does not have the same responsibilities, accountability, or skill set that an urban school principal is expected to have or needs.

The view from the principal's seat is a bit different from the view of other staff members, parents, and community members. In my 20+ years in education, I have had the privilege of serving in positions that have provided me with all perspectives, from the classroom to the district office, as a parent, and as nonprofit organizational support. Nevertheless, the calling to be an urban school principal is not an easy one, but Imagine That—I accepted the challenge!

I want the reader of this book to understand that the stories contained within (which are from a variety of settings) are just snapshots of the stories and struggles that I, as well as other educators in any setting, can tell you about. So, when I say Imagine That, that is what I mean. Imagine that you were the principal. Imagine your reaction and imagine the things that all educators encounter minute by minute, in a classroom of around 20+ students, or in a school of 200-1,400 students (or more).

Our schools are human-service institutions, and as humans, we can be unpredictable and ever-changing. Educators are humans too! Please keep this in mind while reading my words. So, I ask you to sit back, come with me on my journey into my reality of school principalship, and know that we make mistakes too. IMAGINE THAT!

## Chronicle 1 - That Time With a Kid . . .

Just a little information for you! It was rare for me to take a day off because of the number of things that I must deal with when I returned was just not worth taking the time. But I always encouraged colleagues, and had to teach myself, to take the mental health days (paid time off-aka PTO) that were allotted. With anything in life, if you do not take care of yourself, you won't be able to take care of anyone else. No one can pour into others when they are depleted. So, on this day I am about to speak of, I was supposed to be off work. I thank the Lord that I decided to stop by and make sure that everything was ok.

Unannounced, I walked into the office around 10 am that day. I made my rounds and said hello to everyone. Some looked side eyed, while others looked a bit surprised, because they knew that I was supposed to be off. I don't mind letting staff know when I will be out of the building because it gives others a leadership opportunity. I checked in with the administrative assistant to make sure everything was ok, and she gave me an update on the classrooms. Ms. James, a food service worker, was in a tizzy, as usual, about something a student did at breakfast even though the breakfast monitors took care of the situation. Mr. Noel was already having discipline issues with his 6th grade class; walking them down the hallway to PE class was always a sight to see. And then there was Ms. Tannen. Ms. Tannen was a first year (first grade) teacher from a suburban area who had never worked in a predominantly black school (even as a preservice teacher in college). Although she was not trained to work in the setting she was in, Ms. Tannen handled her classroom like a Boss—21 students, 12 on IEPs (Individualized Educational Plans), and probably a few more that had not been identified yet, and needed IEPs. As a first-year teacher, she met my expectations. She was always willing to learn, asking questions, and implementing the feedback that I or the instructional coach would provide.

On this particular day, one student was off the chain, (meaning behaviorally challenged), and she tried everything in her toolbox to get him back on track. The struggle was real. At 10 in the morning, she had already called the office twice for help with this student. Typically, this student would calm down when he saw me. He knew if he made it to my office that it was the last stop on his ride. So, I decided to visit her classroom. I wanted him and the other students to see my face.

Walking down the hallways in a school of over 1,000 students was always a sight to see. It was such a huge school and so much for students and adults to explore. Anything from kids running down the hall, walking out without permission, to students cussing could be transpiring. And that is definitely not an exhaustive list. *Imagine That!* Always an adventure! I rounded the corner to Ms. Tannen's room, as her classroom is adjacent to the students' restrooms. As I rounded the corner, I heard a crackling noise not unlike drywall cracking. I slowed down in front of the girls' restroom and it stopped. I couldn't hear it anymore, so I made my way, slowly, towards the boys' restroom next door. One step, I heard the sound again, looked up, and then CRASH!!!

I was in a daze. However, I opened my eyes to look up again, and a security guard was asking if I was alright. I was on the floor with some freaking white stuff in my eyes, crap all over my clothes, and something moving around on top of me. I pushed the moving thing off me, and the security guard pulled me up to my feet. While he was asking if I was ok, I quickly interrupted him (forgetting where I was for a moment) not even looking to see what I just pushed off me. "What the hell just happened?" I asked. "Look!" he said, turning me around to see what was balled up on the floor behind me. It was Ms. Tannen's problem child of the day. Ain't that a b*&^%! (I said that about 50 times a day **to myself** by the way). I pulled down on my face like I was in a haunted house and screaming at the top of my lungs. Instead of screaming, I said, "You have got to be kidding me!" as most of us do when something so unbelievable has happened.

I asked Officer Simmons to pick the tiny human up and take him to the Nurse. I wanted to make sure that the student was ok. I also wanted the officer and the nurse to get an initial statement from the student. Many times, when students come to their senses, they will change their story to try to not get in trouble. *Imagine That!*

Luckily, I grabbed my radio before leaving the office, so I radioed the head custodian, Mr. Mosby, to come to the hallway. A cleanup needed to be done quickly before the lunch hours started and heavy traffic was coming through the hallways. As I was waiting on Mr. Mosby, I took pictures of everything. By the time he got there, Officer Simmons was back and told me to come into the boys' restroom. He stated that the student said something about climbing up on the toilet to get into the ceiling. I will be damned if it wasn't true. Officer Simmons took pictures of the damage done to the ceiling which showed the student had pushed out and broken a few tiles. Apparently, he climbed up on the toilet and partition to get into the ceiling. Once in the ceiling, it looked like he broke a few tiles and kept crawling trying to get to his classroom. The student told the officer he just wanted to scare the kids in his class. This child was a little different. I'm just sayin'.

Let me remind you, this is a 6-7-year-old student that decided to take it upon himself to scare his classroom. At the expense of his own life, and health, he did what he thought was the best thing to do to accomplish his goal. This is not uncommon in the 6-7-year-old male mind. As the saga continued, more details came to light. Ms. Tannen stated that she let the student go to the restroom. Her gut feeling told her not to, but he was dancing in his seat. She typically timed her students, but today she was exhausted by this time and totally forgot. I've been there, it happens! She was just about to send another student to check on him when she heard the noise in the hallway. Ms. Tannen stepped out and saw it was him on top of ME! I had no idea and did not recall this, but she did see the security officer coming down the hallway towards us and asked if I was alright. She then told him that she would call the office.

But here comes the good part, meeting with the parents! For a school principal/administrator, meeting with the parents can be a source of stress. Many times, we have to convey unpleasant news to parents and believe me, we don't like it either. Coming to the principal's office as a kid or adult is usually not a comfortable experience. Even as a school principal, I felt some type of way walking into my daughter's principal's office. It just wasn't something that I ever enjoyed, although I personally didn't have really bad school experiences as a child. So, I can't imagine what it is like for parents and kids that have had unpleasant experiences. However, I tried my best to make parents and students feel comfortable and good when coming to my office. It did not always have to be a bad thing. Reality was, though, most times it was. Just know if you are uncomfortable, your school principal may be as well. They are just trying to do their job and do what is best for all students in the school. The focus cannot be on just yours alone like it can be at home. What is a principal to do? (Throws hands up). Now . . . back to the story.

Meeting with the "ceiling" child's parents was remarkably interesting. When the administrative assistant called to let them know that I needed to speak with them immediately, and in person, there were questions before they even hit the door. I tried my best to coach my assistant on how to give parents information, but not all the information. The most important information being that there was an incident, and your child is in the nurse's office at this time. It is best that they hear it from me along with the options for consequences. In the end, talking with them face to face is the option that I preferred. Then I could have witnesses for the meeting, talk to them about the statements that were given, and if they wanted to hear their child's side, they could do that too. Over the phone gets too messy. Seeing as I was one of the people directly involved in the "fall" I wanted them to see the damage to the school, his body, and my body as well. Before the parents arrived, I made sure to have statements from all the staff members involved, along with my own. I reviewed discipline policy to determine consequences for this type of behavior and copied it for the parents to see. In other words, I made sure to have all my ducks in a row! Meetings and conversations on the fly are a daily occurrence but for meetings like this, you need to have your "ish" together. You never know how it will play out. In the age of social media and lawsuits for anything, educators need to be super-duper careful about their communications with everyone. This means students, parents, and community. The way that our society treats and looks at educators is not necessarily in the best way. It has been my experience that there are other countries that admire their educators and treat them like royalty, but this has been like a pendulum in the United States! It seems that educators are held accountable for all the evils of society, as if they had a part in what can be seen as the violent and degrading foundation of this country. It is amazing. Oh, sorry, I did it again.

The parent meeting began with the niceties of asking about their day, and thanking them for coming in so quickly to see about their son. Then I went into the events of the day, starting with the teacher's account for the morning during the time that I was not there, all the way until I was blindsided by the "fallen." I also shared with them the staffs' statements, building pictures, and the possible aftermath of bodily pains that he and I may have after this (we both were checked out by the nurse). When I was finished, the parents wanted to bring their son into the office. I had a gut feeling this was not gonna be good, but I allowed it. The next few minutes were a confirmation of why this student thought that it would be okay to scare his class in this way. I was informed by the parents that two days prior to this incident, the student was crawling in the attic in his home and playing with his older brother. Although he did not get hurt at home, he did however, get thoroughly cussed out by his mother for hiding from her in the attic and not coming when she called his name to clean the dishes. Well, his teacher was not going to be able to do that! So, he thought it would be fun to hide and possibly scare his teacher and classmates. I mean, his teacher can't cuss him out or touch him, right? Not to mention the ceiling could not hurt him. So, in his mind it was a no brainer. Let's do this!

Imagine that, the cursing out by his mother occurred again in my office. It was worse after the parents asked me what his consequences were, because he received out of school suspension for his behavior. So, the father joined in with some disciplinary measures of his own. I felt bad. My body ached a bit from the moving mass that hit me in my head and floored me. But my heart ached more for the student. All the staff that interacted with this student knew that something wasn't connecting (cognitively that is). I tried my best to reiterate to the parents that maybe the testing that we had been suggesting all year needed to take place now. Incidents like this are not only dangerous to him but for other staff and students as well. As we can see! But it was a no go. They just felt he was being defiant and silly. Boys will be boys! (That phrase just burns my behind) *Imagine That!*

*Parent Pointers . . .*

The phrase "Boys will be boys!" is not a suitable response to your child's behavior. The behavior that a child displays at home is not always appropriate in a school. Just as your behavior, as an adult, may need to be modified when you enter certain settings (your job, your parent's home, department store, a doctor's office, a courtroom, etc.). Your child's behavior needs to be aligned with the expectations of the educational institution that they attend. There are other people's children in a classroom. He/she is not alone in this educational space. Respecting others, being responsible for their behavior, and being safe are paramount when attending school. Excuses for inappropriate behavior are not acceptable. What you may feel is ok at home, may not be ok at school. Aligning your at-home behavior expectations with the expectations at school is the easiest way to go. It also provides consistency and routine for your child. He/She needs that!

Many school staff members try their best to work with you and your children in this area on a daily basis. Please take the time to partner with your child's teacher(s) and principal. They are there to help him/her to be successful. Be realistic about what you are asking them to do; they can't raise your child for you. But they can support you with creating a plan to help your child become more successful behaviorally and academically. Just like you feel like you can't do it all, they feel the same. It's a partnership! Imagine that!

## Chronicle 2 - That Time When a Parent . . .

It was a typical spring Friday at the charter school where I worked. The birds were chirping, teachers were coming in with smiles on their faces, the students were half-asleep walking through the doors, and the sun was shining through our large glass windows that went from the ceiling to the ground. My duty post was at the front door and it has been in almost every school that I have worked. Greeting the students, staff, and parents in the morning as they walked into the school always gave me insight into who/what might be an issue for the day. Parents had access to talk to me and it made me visible for people to see I was in the building. It also provided students the opportunity to engage with me daily if they wanted to because they knew I existed. I not only stood at the front door during arrival, but I was there for dismissal as well. This is especially important to me as a leader. Being visible in the building holds down a lot of mess. That is the best way I can say it. Consistency in being visible, available, and present are the things, I believe, that contributed to the success that I have had in my leadership positions. People crave consistency and predictability in many situations. For staff, parents, and students to know that you possess (and show that you possess) these characteristics is very helpful to gaining investment from them. You can't just talk the talk; you have to walk the walk! All that lip service does not work, never will! I will stop. Now . . . back to the story.

With over 900 students, upwards of 100 staff members, and any number of parents filtering in and out during arrival, I always heard that breakfast in the cafeteria was no less than highly entertaining. But due to my being posted at the front door every morning, I rarely made it there to engage. Especially on Friday mornings. The impending weekend always brings another element to the school week. Even though I stated to everyone entering the school that it was a Fabulous Friday, it quickly turned into a Freaky Friday on this day. As I finished the morning announcements, I was immediately approached by three of the cafeteria staff members that were a bit frustrated with a few of the 7th grade young ladies that morning at breakfast. These three scholars had been a consistent issue for the 6th-8th grade principal for a good part of this school year. The cafeteria ladies said that they were disrespectful, cursed at them, and took food from other students when they could not get the items that they wanted. One of the girls threatened to have her mom come up and beat one of the cafeteria ladies' ASSETS (if you know what I mean). Yeah! She said it just like that in front of everyone. Several of the staff members on duty, along with a large group of students, confirmed the events that the cafeteria staff brought to me. Of course, I had to get statements. The students were rude, disrespectful, and noticed by a lot of the students and staff in the cafeteria. I am a leader that does not in any way tolerate disrespect of anyone. That could be staff to students, students to staff, staff to parents, etc. This event was just totally uncalled for and had to be addressed. So, I took some time to gather all the information that I needed. In the meantime, I put in a call to all the girls' parents. By the time that I was finished, the young ladies were supposed to go to lunch. I requested that a security officer escort them to get their food from the cafeteria and then be brought to my office (we had six officers by the way—this will be important later).

Now, let me give you a little background about this school. It was a huge building, with many doors and windows. The number of points of entry in this school was ridiculous, and I do not think anyone thought about this when it was being renovated. They just wanted it to be updated, big and pretty to attract families to the school. Safety was one of our biggest concerns all day, every day. And with so many students in the school, the hiding places and entry/exit points were even more of a headache for our officers to be able to control. Thus, the beginning of a nightmare . . .

The security guard brought the girls to my office with their trays. They sat down in my office and I, along with their assistant principal, began talking about their actions in the cafeteria that morning. I told them about the data that I had collected, and the possible consequences that they could have because of their behavior. Everything was going the way it should have gone. Then over my radio I heard, **"We have a breach of security in the cafeteria. All security needed at this time to the cafeteria! NOW!!!"** I thought to myself, *you have got to be F^&#$()@ kidding me!* The Assistant Principal and I left the girls in the office with my secretary. I alerted her to call the police, as we ran down the hallway to the cafeteria. Now just picture it: 400 kids in the cafeteria (6th-8th graders); six security officers; two administrators; three custodians; three cafeteria workers, and three unknown adults fighting the three cafeteria workers. Yes! *Imagine That*! The teachers came down to try to gather kids after they heard about the chaos (thank God). The other principal and I tried to clear out the cafeteria. Meanwhile, the adult fighting ensued. The security guards restrained two parents, while one parent was getting molly-whopped (beat down) by a cafeteria worker. Nobody could stop that one; even the one available security guard couldn't step in on it because he felt like he would have hurt one of the women trying to end it. Therefore, it just kept going until the parent was laying on the floor and basically had tapped out. The cafeteria worker, shouting some expletives at the parent, told her, "That's what yo' a-- get, you didn't know what you was walkin' into, did you?" By this time the police were there, and they handcuffed all of the intruders. Freakin' Unreal!

Sitting the intruders down on the floor handcuffed, the police officers began to ask for statements from the staff members that were still there. To my surprise, our three intruders were relatives of one of the students that were sitting in the office at the time. A friend of the students' opened one of the three side cafeteria doors for the adults to get in. Then the adults approached the staff members that they thought they were going to show "what it is" that day. I came to find out that one of the students called her mother after the incident, and basically lied to her about how the events that happened. If the mother would have called me back before coming up to enter the school illegally, she would have heard the other sides to the story; not just her daughter's side. It continues to amaze me how some parents don't even want to hear the feedback from school staff about their children. With some parents there is just no trust there and no matter what the school staff does, they don't believe in them. Not even thinking or considering the fact that kids will tell their side of the story knowing how their parents will react because they have seen them pop off before with school staff. In other words, kids know how to push their parents' buttons, and sometimes they will use that to their advantage. They will tell teachers all about their parents and the things they see them say/do at home. Then go home and tell their parents what their teachers/principals did. Kids using their influence to trigger parents to go against educators/the school? You really believe this doesn't happen, huh? How about you make an agreement with the educators in your child's school; you can believe 50% of what your kids say about them, if they believe 50% of what your kids say about you? We all will be better for it! *Imagine That!*

*Parent Pointers . . .*

Yes, you would like your home to be like Vegas, what happens there stays there. BUT, that is not the reality of life. Students will come to school and spill all the beans about what's going on at home because they have found people that they feel they can trust and talk to. It's ok, they need these outlets and ways to vent or share their feelings. And many times, if there is a safety issue, the educators in the school will alert you or the appropriate authorities (as they are mandated reporters). However, there is a flip side to this. Because students are embarrassed or ashamed of their behavior at school, many times they will try to cover up or blame others when they are caught or get in trouble.

So, when your student brings home information, or calls you from school, I beg you to speak with a school administrator or teacher before you jump to conclusions. We all know that the default setting in every human is to NOT tell on ourselves. That's just fact! Poppin' off with school staff in front of students is not the way to go. It shows the highest level of disrespect and it gives the child the idea that you are against the school and its staff. This opens the door for more conflict and for your child to not have a good school experience.

It is typical that when adults have had bad school experiences in their past, they communicate these experiences to their children (whether verbally or through their own actions). For the best interest of the child, and your own personal mental health, try your best to presume positive intent. Yes, there are bad apples in every profession. But educators, most times, are not going into education to hurt children. It's because we love children and we want them to be successful adults. Having adversarial relationships with parents is not advantageous for anyone, especially your child. So, when things like this happen, your first line of defense is the classroom teacher, then the principal. We all want to believe what our children say.

Realistically, it's not always the best choice to react to everything they present because it may not be the whole truth. Self-preservation is our survival mechanism. Consequences for our behavior are a constant in life. How we deal with them (good or bad) is most important. Let's teach them how to honorably address their behavior without having to lie or physically harm someone.

## Chronicle 3 - That Time Of Change . . .

Something about this school year was different! I could not put my finger on it. It was a smaller school, smaller staff, and the student population was less than 20% of the school from which I just came. I walked into this school as the new head principal. Nonetheless, there was an interesting feel there; like people were really comfortable with the environment and the lack of achievement that was happening. Anyone who knows me knows that I am a leader that will say off top, "Get comfortable with uncomfortable!" Not because I want to hurt people or make people miserable; it is because I know one of my purposes in life is to grow people in many areas, personally and professionally. However, everyone has an aversion to change, to not being comfortable in situations; whether we want to admit it or not. This school environment needed some change. Don't get me wrong, not everything needed a glow up in the school, but in some particularly important areas, growth was definitely necessary.

Along with a new instructional coach I inherited, I was also charged with hiring three new staff members that would serve on the Leadership Team for the school. Everybody would be learning, and I would definitely be teaching (that's what leaders do). Basically, I had to create a support team in a school where the staff was seasoned (had been there for years, some had been there for decades) and pushing back against anything that they were not already doing. But you know what; I was down for the cause and up for the challenge. However, it excited me to know that they could be so passionate about things. My job was to get them to be just as passionate about change for efficiency and growth in the same way. It was not easy, but by the end of the year it was definitely worth it!

By October of the school year, we had gotten into a rhythm. By December, we were on autopilot and growing like it wasn't nothin! For instance:

1. Three new people were added to our Leadership Team.

2. The staff appeared to be coming around to the "new to them" expectations, routines, and systems put in place.

3. The students and families seemed to be coming on board with the updated operations that our school family was trying to create.

Discipline in the school was one of the areas that we were working hard on. But when students and teachers are not held accountable for their actions, it is a recipe for disaster. Yes, students have a voice. Yes, students are people, too. Yes, students deserve the respect that we ask for and from them. However, they cannot run a school! And in this school, it appeared that at least five students (the highflyers as I call them) were doing just that, before I got there. We all know that once kids see other kids acting a certain way and getting away with it, then they think it's ok to join in the fun as well. This can cause a hell of a problem in a school. Just like anything, it must be addressed consistently and with appropriate consequences if necessary. Many things can be chalked up to the fact that children need modeling and guidance when navigating their behaviors. The adults are another story I will not get into. But some things just need plain ole consequences. If we do not give them to children, at some point life will, and it will most likely be harsher than what we provide. Consequences for your choices come naturally in life, whether good or bad. Children need to understand this in their younger years so that when they are adults, they will be better able to handle conflicts if someone tells them no or won't let them do what they want to do. It is my belief that many of our harsher consequences in adulthood come from issues not being addressed in our childhood. Nobody taught us! As a parent myself, I understand the pain that we have providing consequences for our kids. But the way that I feel is that I would rather give my child a consequence than have someone else or life give it to them later. At least I can control the consequence and know that I am not hurting my child, degrading my child, or scarring them for life. I don't know what life or someone else would do. So, I would rather teach my child myself. *Imagine That!*

Leadership/Teacher Tips . . .

For Leaders walking into a building where the culture/climate is not what you would like it to be:

1)     Be Consistent—Consistency creates safety (emotional, physical and psychological) and boundaries for behavior.

2)     Inspect what you Expect—Clarity is key, know what you want, communicate it and look for it. If you don't see it, remind people consistently and move to consequences if necessary.

3)     Don't Deny Your Gangsta—You cannot cure anything you don't confront. As leaders you have to have the courage

to confront things that are not proficient, effective, or appropriate. Leadership is not for the weak at heart. It does not serve anyone well when a leader cannot step up to the plate in tough times and be a truth teller. If you don't create the culture/climate, it will create itself.

For Teachers in a building where the culture/climate is not what you would like it to be:

1) Your classroom is located in the larger environment of a school. Just because you feel your classroom environment is good, that doesn't mean you just get to say to H-E double hockey sticks with the rest of the

school. You and your students have to come to the school every day and feel that climate. You are not held up in your classroom room the entire day. Why wouldn't you want the school to be the best that it can be for every student, parent, teacher, etc. that walks into it? Step up and say something to your colleagues! Period!

2)    You know when your colleagues are not proficient at what they do. As a professional we all should be held accountable for our performance. If you see or hear a colleague not doing what they are supposed to do or treating a student badly, you need to speak on it.

For some reason teachers are quick to report an administrator, but they won't report that teacher in Room 10 that they hear yell at kids every day, talk to parents badly, sitting at their desk all day and not teaching, etc. Why is this? If you are so concerned about the administrator, why wouldn't you be just as (or more) concerned about a teacher who is in a classroom all day with a group of children? I'm perplexed.

3)   Speak your truth! We have become a social media society where we go on social media to complain, cry, show our new whips, etc. Don't do this when it comes to school issues. It's just not a

good idea. Many school districts have technology policies now that restrict what you can post on social media, and you could possibly be terminated from your position because of it. If you want to speak to someone, and you have school administration that listens, please go to your leadership team first. Social media is not a way to solve the problems at your school.

## Chronicle 4 - That Time With the Fire . . .

My Chronicle 3 words lend themselves to the story that you are about to read. Whether you agree or not, maybe you will reflect a little more on your stance when you finish. Well, let us proceed.

Fall days in the Midwest are absolutely beautiful! The leaves on the trees have turned all types of bright colors; the air is crisp enough to wear a long-sleeved shirt, but still no jacket because it might be hot later, and there is a newness in the air; kind of like how you feel when you are going through a good transition in your life. Anyway, it's awesome!

The school was abuzz because we were having morning assembly (which we did every Monday) but it was the beginning of a new month. We always celebrated our perfect attendance (for staff and students), academic accomplishments, birthdays for the month and anything else we could think of on the first Monday of the month. It was something for everyone to look forward to. We always had fun, took a lot of pictures, and talked about our expectations for the next 30 days.

The morning assembly went very well. Our instructional coach decided she wanted to take over that month and plan the whole thing. Which was fine with me! She did an awesome job. I felt bad going after her the next week (LOL). During the assembly, I checked in with the highflyers (kids that typically have behavior issues). I liked to do this in the morning during arrival, but I did not see them all for some reason. They were all in the assembly, though. Ironically, three were receiving perfect attendance awards. Honestly, it seems that the ones that you don't really want to see every day always come to school. A caveat to that is no student could receive perfect attendance if they were suspended at any time during the previous 30 days. So, for us, it was a win because these three highflyers came to school every day. However, we cannot say without incident, but they did not get suspended in the previous month. They made it through the first two and a half months of school without suspension.

---

**Side Note**: For any educator reading this, did you know that October is the month when the true colors of our students come out? In my experience, the highest number of suspensions usually happen in October (the honeymoon is over), January (after holiday break) and April (after state testing).

---

By October, the students usually have felt you out since the first day of school. They get comfortable with you by then and the expected behavior they have shown you, possibly, cannot last any longer (the representative can't fake it any longer). Sounds kind of like when you are dating someone, huh? Ok, that's another topic, let's go back!

The morning assembly kicked off our day/week in a fantastic way. The school was bustling, and the energy was super positive. Until . . . something came over my radio. The freakin' radio, I tell ya! "MC1 come in please." We used codes for our radio transmissions so no one who heard them would know who we were talking to. I learned to do this in my previous school. Eventually staff learned them, but it took a while. "Go for MC1." "MC1 I need your assistance in the cafeteria hallway." Thinking to myself, *the damn cafeteria!* "Copy, MC1 on the way." I get to the cafeteria hallway and the Behavior Specialist, Mr. Jacobs, is there. He tells me that one of our highflyers was allowed to go to the restroom and had not returned to the classroom yet. He looked for him in the two male student restrooms that we had, and he wasn't there. So, he was wondering if I could go into the girls' restrooms and look. He heard some sounds in the restroom and did not want to walk in on anyone. I totally agreed. I walked into the girl's restroom at the front of the school. There were girls in there. I stayed in with them until they walked out, and I checked all of the stalls. Nobody else was in there. Walking to the back of the school (the school was one level with long hallways) we then began to hear some commotion and smelled a stench. It smelled like something burning. So, we pick up the pace and once again, I find myself running. I'm thinking, *Man, I'm glad I do interval training*! The smell gets stronger as we get down the hallway and when the custodian meets us, he starts running as well. While running we pass a fire alarm, and the custodian pulls it. I didn't even stop to ask why. In hindsight, I get it! I had stressed safety so much that he was doing what was best at that time. My mind was on finding out the source of the problem. As we get closer to the restroom, we see smoke coming out of the door and a small figure darting down the hallway. The Behavior Specialist continues after the figure while the whole school is exiting as if it were a routine fire drill. The custodian and I go into the girl's restroom, where the smoke is coming from, and almost run into a trash can ON FIRE! You can already guess what I was saying to myself, right? The custodian and I literally said it out loud at the same time (WTF). We did not know what was on fire, what was put in the trash can, or anything. But when I say this is the only time in my career that the fire department came right away, I mean the ONLY time. The Lord was with us, and we were grateful! Not even one minute after stepping into the bathroom, and our WTF revelation, a firefighter came in with an extinguisher and put the fire out. He sprayed the floor, the can, the wall, the ceiling, everything in and around the trash can to make sure that nothing spread. The smoke from the trash can was awful. It was everywhere and as we exited the bathroom, we all smelled like smoke. Later that evening, I had to throw those clothes and shoes away. Also, the little hair that I had on my head stank so bad, I wanted to pull it out (LOL).

In the meantime, the police showed up as well, not like I am not familiar with working with them at this point! They were asking questions, just as the firemen were, and trying to find out what happened. Giving and recording/writing statements seemed to be my life (something that grad school did not teach me, by the way), but trying to figure this out while answering 20 questions began to get extremely frustrating.

Who was that running out of the bathroom as we were coming around? Did Mr. Jacobs catch him? Where the hell is he? What on God's green earth possesses someone to set a trash can on fire in a school full of people? All these questions were running through my mind when another police officer, the behavior specialist, and the "fire" kid walked up. HERE was the culprit! While speaking to the officer and Mr. Jacobs, I was informed that the student broke down and confessed to the crime just after Mr. Jacobs caught him outside of the front doors trying to run through students that were exiting the building. First, he tried to blame it on another student, of course! Then, as the police officer was talking about handcuffing him and sitting him in the police car, he began to cry and confess. The highflyer "fire kid" was actually scared. What? After you set a trash can on fire in a school full of people? *Imagine That!*

When I tell you that if you knew the rap sheet that this second grader had before I got to the school, you would not be surprised by this behavior. He already had a DJO (Deputy Juvenile Officer) that I hadn't met yet because I guess they felt he was doing so well that he didn't need a check in—until now! Unfortunately, this young man was troubled in more ways than one. I came to discover that one of his offenses, while in kindergarten, involved setting a room on fire in his grandmother's home, while the family was asleep. His grandmother was his legal guardian because his mother and father were both incarcerated and previously on drugs. He lived with his grandmother and uncles, which meant that he was around adults all day. He was constantly roaming the neighborhood at all times of the day and night doing what he wanted to do. Basically, living his best life it seemed. It was not the case.

Nevertheless, this year, for some reason, he had not had any issues until now. The previous year, he had been suspended three to four times by this time of the school year. He had no suspensions since I took over the building—until now! The process for giving consequences for this young man would be a long one. Even though it was a violation of a federal law to start a fire on school grounds, he had a therapist, a DJO, and a caseworker that I had to communicate and plan with regarding how to get him some help while also protecting the school community. I can't tell you everything that had to go into this, but it was definitely a learning experience for me and him. I didn't want him removed from an environment and a teacher that he was doing well with until this incident. I believed the trigger that caused him to set the fire was instilled in him from birth. He acted as if he had seen things in his short, young life that many adults probably wouldn't have been able to handle. However, in the end, he did receive consequences and came back to school on a part-time basis until we saw some improvement in his behavior. The adults, including myself, in this situation needed to be consistent in the support that we provided for him as well. This helped to build trust between him and adults. The trauma he endured may have caused him to not trust adults, and one way that he knew how to control his circumstances was to be able to play with fire. He knew it scared others, but it did not scare him. Ultimately, he said the only reason he ran was because he didn't want to get in trouble with his teacher. He liked her and was going to let her know what he did. So, if you ever hear about relationships being key in order to educate children, *Imagine That!*

Leadership/Teacher Tips . . .

Relationships are KEY in every facet of our lives. No one progresses through this life alone. From birth we are wired to attach to or detach from things, people and experiences in our lives. Learning how to have healthy relationships is one of the hardest things to do throughout our lives. What is healthy to one person may not be healthy to another. This takes work, grace, patience, and a lot of other traits to develop in concert with other parties.

When we find children that may have some attachment deficiencies, as the adults we have to take the lead on showing them that we can be trusted and we are there to support them in healthy ways. If parents/guardians don't want to work with you to get help for the student, do as much that is in YOUR power to do during the school day. Whether that is to advocate for more IEP minutes, behavioral health services, doubling up on in school/outside counseling, more frequent personal check-ins, etc. In the end, we are responsible for the students in our building while they are with us. That means treating them just as good as you would want your own child to be treated. If it weren't for the children in our schools every day, we wouldn't have our jobs. Let's be mindful of our WHY on a daily basis!

The student spoken about in this chronicle ended up being one of the top performers in the school that year, academically. Although his behavior was not always the best, he created an attachment to his teacher and the leadership team that he never had before. He didn't know how to navigate that or trust that in the beginning. In reality, the old him was beefin' with the new him. The behavioral supports and wraparound services that we put in place for him helped him immensely in one short year.

The next school year he ended up at another school, due to family transition, and the process had to begin again. This happens a lot in urban demographic schools. It didn't work out too well for him there and I wonder every school year where he is now. In the end, I know that we (the leadership team, school staff, and support services) did everything we could for that young man. I'm proud of him for the progress that he made. I truly hope that he is in a healthier/safer living and psychological situation today.

## Chronicle 5 - That Time With Vibe Guy . . .

Much of my educational career has been at the elementary level. If you have ever walked in an elementary school you might have noticed that the staff typically is composed of all women. However, for two years now there were at least five members (10%) of our school staff that were male teachers. It was refreshing, but also challenging. Challenging in the sense that when females in an elementary school see a man, it's like dangling a coffee gift card in front of them on the Monday morning after Spring Break (LOL). If you do not know the feeling, just think about your favorite food/drink that looks so good to you even when you know you shouldn't have it. Forbidden feels sooooo good, doesn't it? Got it now? Good!

In many of my experiences, many school districts did not have written policies regarding dating/hooking up with another employee that works in your school. If they did, it really wasn't enforced. But as a school administrator, I highly discourage it because I know what can happen in the end. It is a recipe for disaster. The hurt feelings, arguments, and backlash that can come from two staff members relating outside of school can affect the work that they do when they come to work. When everything is ok, it's all good! However, when things go bad, it can be all bad! I have seen couples argue, fuss, and literally fight in school hallways, the teacher's lounge, and on the school parking lot. Whether the students are there or not, it's of no matter to them when the emotions get high. Like my cousin says, "When keepin' it real goes WRONG." In addition, if you are a school principal that hangs out with your staff, you may hear/see things, and drinking only intensifies the situations.

You want to hear about it? Here we go! Supervising men and supervising women in a school is different in some ways. Women seem to be a bit more emotional about things, and may communicate differently. I am not saying anything is wrong with that; we are created differently. However, supervising men, for me, is a bit easier. They want information in a straightforward manner. Give them the assignment, be clear about it, and they do it.

Early on in my career a semi-mentor told me, "Never date anyone that you work with!" Of course, I didn't understand why, and being in the schools that I was in for so long, that would not have happened anyway. The staffs were predominantly women, and any men that I saw I wasn't interested in anyway (they weren't my type). Although I may have dated someone from another school or within the same school district, I didn't even come close to "the forbidden."

Until this distinct school year, 15 years into my career, I had never been tempted to even hang out with the people that I worked with. This staff, however, was different. I could chill with this staff; they were cool people. They understood the line between personal and business, and we all had some similar interests outside of education that created a vibe unlike any of the other group of teachers that I had encountered. Within this group was a male teacher that I totally vibed with. He and I hit it off when I walked into the building my first year there. For a year and a half, we talked to, supported, and intrigued each other.

At the conclusion of a parent teacher conference day, the staff decided that they wanted to blow off some steam and go partake in some day drinking since it was a Friday. They invited me to join them, but I could not go at the time that they were leaving. Even though they were finished with conferences and their day was over, mine was not. So, I told them that I would stop by the bar that they were going to and see if they were still there when I was finished.

A few hours later, I was finished and leaving the school. Funny thing is, in my gut I did not even want to go to where my colleagues may have been. But I went anyway.

---
**Side Note**: Always go with your gut!
---

I stepped into the bar and looked around. I did not see anyone. Then I asked the bartender if he knew where the group of teachers from the school might be. He immediately smiled and knew the group (I was not surprised because they were memorable). Then he told me that they were at the bar, which was on the other side of the wall. I was really hoping that he told me he didn't know them, and I would have gladly gone home. But, before I left the bar he asked, "Are you their principal?" I looked at him slyly and said, "Yeeessss, why do you ask?" He started chuckling and said, "Oh, nothing bad, they were just talking about you and had some funny stories, that's all. I just wanted to know if you were the Drill Sergeant, the super cool principal they were talking about." I laughed out loud. If you have ever heard me laugh, you know it's loud! I know that the people I work with talk about me, but I also feel it's none of my business what they think. I told the bartender that I hope they didn't talk too bad about me and thanked him for babysitting them today. Hopefully, I can take over now.

I walked around the wall and saw that only four people were left out of the group of eleven. One of them was my "vibe" buddy. He was sitting at the end of the bar when I walked in. They all threw their hands up when I walked in, and yelled, "JOHNSON!" That's just what we did when we were out. So, I sat down next to my guy. Funny, didn't know he was going to be that "for real" at the time. Anywho, I sat down, and he ordered me a drink. He had committed to memory the different alcohols that I could drink. Nice touch on his part.

---

Side Note: Did I forget to mention I had a hellified amount of food and alcohol allergies at this time? It was the worst!

---

We started talking with each other first. He asked me how the rest of the day went. We discussed some craziness going on with some parents, etc. Then, another staff member asked if they could join in the top-secret conversation. So, I told them the same thing that I told vibe guy (I could only tell them so much as an administrator; not everything). The conversations bounced back and forth from one end of the bar to the other until it was just vibe guy and me, single and free. I know right? This just got interesting.

The night at the bar turned into breakfast in the morning. Nooooo, we didn't do that! Not yet at least. But it definitely was a turning point in the administrator-teacher relationship that we had. Leaving him after breakfast felt as if I had to part from a best friend. As I was driving home, I felt "all the things" from head to toe. The sun was shining, and I was on a cloud, totally into this man. Quickly, the sunny day turned to rain. Talking to myself: *What the hell are you doing? This is one of the teachers in a school that you lead! Heffa, are you crazy? He is your subordinate. You have got to stop this where it is before it gets too far. DO IT NOW!*

The thoughts were dominating my day and the remainder of my weekend. I couldn't shake them. I spoke with vibe guy four more times that weekend. We talked about everything from childhood traumas and memories to adult/family topics. I cannot tell you everything, but let's just say it got deep. You know, those long conversations that take you into the night and possibly early morning when you first start dating someone? Those were our types of conversations. We both seemed to have wanted this for a long time, or at least thought about it. Before you say/think anything sideways, let me say this. I am sure that there has been a situation in your life where it seemed that all things aligned, when you met someone, and there was just that one aspect of the situation that just wasn't quite right. This was that situation. Eighty percent of it was right in my mind/heart, but 20% was super wrong and inappropriate. However, who hasn't done something that they weren't 100% sure about at some point in their life? (Raised hands should be happening right now).

**Side Note**: Educators are people too! We have feelings, urges, frustrations, etc. Don't get it twisted, educators are not perfect, and we cannot live up to the perfect moral standards that society places on us. Society can't live up to their own standards if we are going to be 100! Whether you want to admit it or not, all of us are having human experiences, which are flawed and not at all nice at times. We deal with them the best way we know how, and hopefully when we know better, we do better. Alright, enough of that.

The coming weeks were a bit awkward, as I was trying to keep my distance, and keep it professional during the day. We talked mostly at night. My efforts to keep the conversations light and airy were an epic fail. In the process of learning about him, I learned that he currently had a girlfriend and they were having relationship problems. After that, it made it a bit easier to keep him at a distance. One weekend, I shared that a close friend of mine was having a birthday party at another friend's nightclub. Vibe guy asked if he could meet me at the party. Reluctantly, I agreed, knowing that the party would be filled with people taking pictures and asking questions if they saw me there with someone. I didn't need, or want, that drama. But he was endearing, handsome, charming, and just super sexy. In the back of my mind, I knew he had a girlfriend, but I couldn't resist. Once again, I didn't go with my gut. Take this as a lesson everyone: Do not let your heart live in "the forbidden." Feelings are great servants, but horrible masters!

The party was just what I thought it would be—fancy, crowded, movers and shakers in the house, and the music was bangin! From the DJ to the club owner, I knew so many people in the venue that just thinking about vibe guy being there made me nervous. He texted to say he was on the way, and my heart sank. When he got there, a friend girl and I were standing by the bar, and I saw him walk through the door. We locked eyes and smiled at each other. He came straight over to me, said hello, and gave me a hug. He smelled so good, OMG! Trying to move past the smell, I was glad that he brought a friend because that made the look of everything appear more happenstance-like (is that a word?). Throughout the night, he would come to visit whatever spot my friend and I were hanging in. Typically, when I used to go out, I was on the dance floor all night. But when I became a principal, I had to hold all that down. The possibility of seeing parents, or even former students out, was remarkably high in the city that I lived in. I learned that in a strip club, in a nearby city, one early morning (don't ask!).

Out of the blue the DJ played my favorite song. I think he did it on purpose, but I won't go there. So of course (rolling my eyes), vibe guy asks me to dance.

Whhhyyyyyy, Lord, whyyyyyyy? I have to say it was AWESOMESAUCE, as my niece says. This man could dance with me, move with me, feel the rhythm and me up on the dance floor? (Ha! Did you catch that?) Instead of being on a cloud, I think I was in heaven. I do not know about you all, but a man that can dance is a total turn on to me. It just does something to me! Whew Chile! I gotta cool down right now just thinking about it. Ok, shake it off, shake it off.

The rest of the night was filled with spurts of dancing, socializing, and finally taking a picture which was totally not a good idea. So, we all know how pictures in clubs go, right? A photographer walks up to you, alone or with a group, and asks you, "Would you like to take a picture?" You say yes or no. Then, they tell you where your picture might end up. Well, I knew the photographer and where he worked, but I didn't think that the picture would end up in the paper. Here I go again, not thinking. The freaking picture ended up in a well-known paper, nice and big on the front page, the next week. WHOOOOAAA MAN, and guess who saw it? District office and the whole staff, of course.

CRAAAAAAPPPP! It was such a jacked-up judgment call. But that's what drinking and partying will get you sometimes. I knew the consequences were coming, and I had to devise a plan. How was I going to explain this one? Think Jerri, think!

The following Monday "it" hit the fan as I thought it would. I was ready! My Assistant Superintendent came to me with a newspaper in hand. She had a look on her face as if she felt she had caught me in something. She always seemed like she wanted me to fail. She was not supportive, and behaved as if she didn't even like kids. I was thinking to myself, *take yo messy behind on somewhere!* (Did I just go there, let me move on). She placed the newspaper on my desk, looked at me and said, "What can you tell me about this?" Of course, it was the infamous picture that I didn't think would make its way to the masses. "Well, I can tell you it's a newspaper," I imparted. Yes, I was being sarcastic (this mouth I tell ya!). She looked at me and pursed her lips. I laughed. "It's a picture of two people that were out at a party and were asked, in the middle of a conversation, if they wanted to take a picture." I looked at her in silence. The wait time was irritating her. I loved it! In situations like this the least amount of information you give, the better. I answered her question and that is all that she needed to know. It wasn't a lie. It was the truth; it just wasn't the whole truth. After the wait time, she proceeded to say that this paper was given to her by one of the staff members at my school. I did not ask who it was, I didn't care. I took it as somebody took it personal that they were not in a picture with me (or maybe him). At this point, it's business, not personal. It was a picture! And that's all that she needed to know. She then stated that this could look bad to the rest of the staff. I told her that her concern was completely understood, and that I would address it at the next staff meeting. If she would like to attend, she was welcomed to. No problem!

The next staff meeting was thought-provoking. I addressed the picture with an open and transparent attitude. Bottom line, it was a picture that could have been taken with any staff member that I was talking to at a party. I have had pictures in the paper before with various people. I also let them know that if there was a concern, they could always come to me personally.

However, if they feel the need to go to anyone above my head, they have the right to do what they feel they need to. I had no issue with it because, as they could see, it will come back to me anyway. Only when I am aware of things is when I can address them. You should have seen vibe guy's face during the staff meeting. It was classic. He tried his best not to show any emotion. After the meeting, I received a text that said, "Great job, I think I just fell in love with you! See you tonight?" I texted back, "Thank you, as you should . . . absolutely!" *Imagine That!*

## Leadership Tips...

I know the first thing people will say is, "Well, I would never . . ." Let me tell you something . . . don't EVER say what you WON'T do. If there is anything that life and leadership have taught me, it's that the minute you start to judge someone else for what they did or didn't do, that situation will present itself in your life to test you. You can call it God, Yahweh, Karma, whatever you want, but it will happen. As humans in this thing called life, I would hope that we try our best to live as right as we possibly can.

But I'm just gonna say SH$ take happens! The best advice I can give is to take facts over feelings in every situation that is placed in front of you. The biggest fact of this situation was that I was the <u>l</u>eader of a building, and I made a bad call to follow my heart instead of my brain.

There were some great things that came out of the situation, but in the end there was more bad than good. No losses just lessons! So please take my advice, to the best that you possibly can, DO NOT date a subordinate or anyone that you work closely with in your school.

Not every situation is negative, but my experience has shown me that it's more bad than good. Other situations like this presented themselves later in my career, hopefully, I can tell you about those later.

However, I learned from this experience and I was able to process more logically having gone through it previously. Where we find love is not in our control, but the situations surrounding how we handle it must be processed and dealt with accordingly. Once again, Leadership is not for the faint of heart. Difficult decisions must be made, and we must be the ones to step up and make them. Facts over Feelings!

## Thoughts . . .

As you conclude the reading of this book, I know that some people will ask the question of how these scenarios are specific to an Urban School Principal. Honest answer, they may not be! All I know is that I identify myself as an Urban School Principal when people ask, and I am proud to be that. I worked in schools/districts that were comprised of predominantly students of color for my whole career. The experiences that other principals had, like me, have helped us to thrive in any occupational environment that we chose to venture into after being Urban School Principals. If we chose to stay, and continue the work, it makes us even more adaptable, empathetic, strategic, and all-around better people. I can attest to the fact that it will either toughen you up or it will break you down. I have seen that there is no in between. Once again, you may agree or disagree, but this is my truth, and I can speak it however I want.

The calling to be an Urban School Principal is not an easy one. I thank God for ALL the educators that are in classrooms and schools every day. Just as any other profession, educators should be appreciated, lifted up, and supported. We should not in any way take them for granted. They develop and teach our future doctors, lawyers, tech giants, entrepreneurs, etc. The creation of all professions comes from them. To put it plainly, without them there would be no other professions. Educators are some of the most selfless, caring, and creative people that exist on this Earth. Treat your educators appropriately. They are more precious than gold!

It took me a long time to want to share just a smidgen of the stories that I have about being an Urban School Principal, but I am so happy that I was able to share it with you. Hopefully, as entertaining as some of it may have been, it has caused you to see educators as real people. Now, the teachers and principals that you never thought had lives outside of school or grappled with the life happenings that you see in reality shows, have hopefully become real to you. You ever wonder why they don't have reality shows like, "Real Educators of L.A.?" I think it's because the things that you might see would be a true eye opener that people really won't be able to handle. It gets real in school! As you can see, from administration, kids and teachers, to the parents, stuff happens that people don't necessarily want others to know. Especially in a social media technology world where people hide behind screens and words, feeling as if they don't have consequences. In a school, there is nothing to hide behind. Daily, educators are out there on the front lines. Yes, I feel we are first responders dealing with it all, from mental/behavioral health issues, parent concerns, administrative pressure, community input, etc., which can cause you to not want to deal with anybody, ever again. It all comes down to those people in the school that make the magic happen for children daily, despite the chaos that is going on around them in this world. Our educators are where the rubber meets the road. I am sure that you can think of a teacher or administrator right now that made a difference in your life. I know I can!

So, I will leave you with this! All educators are dealing with their own lives in addition to the multiple lives of the parents, students, and colleagues that they work with/teach/support daily. When thinking about the realities of this world today, just consider that they may make mistakes, too. Educators have the best interest of your child at heart, and they want to enjoy this life with amazing moments while effectively teaching kids so that they can live their best lives, too. Just as you do!

These stories are what have made me who I am today; I wouldn't trade them for anything. I also have many more. In the end, my hope is that this book will ignite the fire of grace that we should give ourselves, our educators, and fellow colleagues on any given day. You never know someone's story or their struggles. We all have them.

*Imagine That* !

## *Your Thoughts . . .*

*Your Thoughts . . .*

_____

_____

_____

_____

_____

_____

_____

_____

_____

_____

_____

_____

_____

_____

_____

_____

_____

_____

_____

_____

_____

*Your Thoughts . . .*

CPSIA information can be obtained
at www.ICGtesting.com
Printed in the USA
LVHW010225030322
712308LV00009B/501

9 781891 282256